Teen Survival Guides

Managing Your Relationships

SARAH EASON

CHERITON
CHILDREN'S BOOKS

Published in 2026 by **Cheriton Children's Books**
1 Bank Drive West, Shrewsbury, Shropshire, SY3 9DJ, UK

© Copyright 2026 Cheriton Children's Books

First Edition

Author: Sarah Eason
Designer: Paul Myerscough
Editor: Kelly Short
Proofreader: Amy Strauss

Picture credits: Cover: Shutterstock/Jose Calsina. Inside: p4: Shutterstock/Rawpixel.com, p5: Shutterstock/Juice Verve, p6: Shutterstock/Fizkes, p7: Shutterstock/BearFotos, p8: Shutterstock/DimaBerlin, p9: Shutterstock/Ground Picture, p11: Shutterstock/Fizkes, p13: Shutterstock/GaudiLab, p14: Shutterstock/Fast Stock, p15: Shutterstock/Olena Yakobchuk, p16: Shutterstock/Prostock Studio, p17: Shutterstock/Gladskikh Tatiana, p19: Shutterstock/Marian Fil, p21: Shutterstock/Fizkes, p22: Shutterstock/Antonio Guillem, p23: Shutterstock/PeopleImages.com/Yuri A, p24: Shutterstock/Halfpoint, p25: Shutterstock/Alessandro Biascioli, p27: Shutterstock/Golden Pixels LLC, p28: Shutterstock/Fizkes, p29: Shutterstock/Alena Ozerova, p30: Shutterstock/Wavebreakmedia, p31: Shutterstock/Daniel M Ernst, p33: Shutterstock/SpeedKingz, p34: Shutterstock/Media Photos, p35: Shutterstock/Adriaticfoto, p36: Shutterstock/Fizkes, p37: Shutterstock/Ground Picture, p38: Shutterstock/Ground Picture, p39: Shutterstock/Fizkes, p41: Shutterstock/Gorodenkoff, p42: Shutterstock/Inside Creative House, p43: Shutterstock/Amir Ridhwan, p44: Shutterstock/Antonio Guillem, p45: Shutterstock/Prostock Studio, p47: Shutterstock/Pheelings Media, p48: Shutterstock/Pixel Shot, p49: Shutterstock/LightField Studios, p50: Shutterstock/Master1305, p51: Shutterstock/SeventyFour, p53: Shutterstock/Perfect Wave, p54: Shutterstock/Oleggg, p55: Shutterstock/Fizkes, p57: Shutterstock/CarlosBarquero, p58b: Shutterstock/Anna Nahabed, p58t: Shutterstock/Fizkes, p59: Shutterstock/Miljan Zivkovic.

All rights reserved. No part of this book may be reproduced in any form without permission of the publisher, except by a reviewer.

Printed in China

Please visit our website,
www.cheritonchildrensbooks.com
to see more of our high-quality books.

Contents

INTRODUCTION
The Relationship Roller Coaster 4

CHAPTER 1
Communication Is Key 6

CHAPTER 2
**You and Your Family:
    A Survival Guide. 14**

CHAPTER 3
School, College, and Work 28

CHAPTER 4
Friendships and the Wider World 42

CONCLUSION
Skills for Life 58

Glossary. 60
Find Out More 63
Index and About the Author. 64

INTRODUCTION
The Relationship Roller Coaster

Let's face it, the teenage years are not easy. Just dealing with the hormone changes that come with puberty can feel like riding a roller coaster. Your body is changing all the time, and it can be hard to get a handle on what is going on. And as if that isn't tough enough, your mind can feel just as wild—up and down with emotions and confusing thoughts. It can feel out of control.

All Change with Relationships

With so much going on, it might be difficult to think about how you relate to others. Yet, this is a key time to get a handle on managing that part of your life and how it is evolving. Your relationships with your parents and siblings are probably changing. Your friendships can change too—some may grow stronger, while others may fall away. As you and your friends grow up, your interests and personalities will likely develop, and that can also affect friendships. And here's the thing—that doesn't change once the teen years are over. Your relationships will change and grow as you and your life change and grow too. But how you manage your relationships is key. And that's where relationship skills come in.

STUDIES IN TEEN SURVIVAL

Adolescence is a time of huge change—physically, mentally, and emotionally. At this time, people are trying to figure out their identities, what they believe in, and what their values are. They might be more impulsive than ever, and hormones can make moods go up, down, up, down, and up again! All this can make keeping and forming healthy relationships feel like very hard work.

Your relationships can bring a lot of happiness into your life. It makes sense to work on them.

Just like learning a work skill, you can learn relationship skills too.

Skills for Life

You might be thinking, "Why do I need to learn relationship skills? I'm managing my relationships just fine." That may well be true, but most people find that at some stage of their lives, relationships become tricky to deal with. Having some key skills can make all the difference in how you relate to others, and that helps keep your relationships healthy. So, let's get to the skills! Here are ten key relationship tools that we'll explore in this book:

- **Communication**
- **Conflict resolution**
- **Compromise**
- **Assertiveness**
- **Collaboration**
- **Empowerment**
- **Empathy**
- **Tolerance**
- **Respect**
- **Trust-building**

We'll explain what these terms mean as we work through the book and explore them in workshops. And here's some more good news, these skills will help you navigate almost every area of your future—master them, and you can master just about anything that life throws your way.

CHAPTER 1

Communication Is Key

Top of the relationship skills list is communication—it's a deal-breaker when it comes to managing our relationships. Here's why: Effective communication allows people to hear and understand each other's feelings, needs, and perspectives. When people communicate well, they connect, and that makes a relationship work.

Not Always Easy

While communication may be essential for healthy and happy relationships, sometimes it can feel hard to communicate well with the people you care about. Often, because you care, emotions can run high and you may not express yourself well. Sometimes, you can feel really angry during a discussion with a family member or friend.

> Believing that you know the thoughts and feelings of another person without actually asking them what they are thinking and feeling can also lead to a lot of misunderstandings. By talking to them, you can learn what they are truly thinking.

Taking time out to talk is important.

Charging headlong into a furious exchange of words might feel like a load off to start with, but afterward, you are likely to feel bad and regret it. Other times, rather than having an angry exchange of words, you might instead ignore the person you are upset with. Unfortunately, that is often when problems can build up and start to get out of control.

Finding Time to Talk

We all lead busy lives today and often, finding time to sit, talk, and listen to someone can be difficult. But taking the time to communicate properly is effective time management. It will stop problems building that will then take more time to resolve in the long term. It is important to remember to ask other people how they feel and what they think, and to listen carefully to their replies. They will appreciate it too.

Teen Need to Know

People communicate in nonverbal ways as well as verbally. Paying attention to body language helps you learn a lot more about what other people are thinking and feeling than just listening to words alone.

Let's Talk about Communication

The key to effective communication is keeping the pathways of communication flowing. That means making the effort to talk to the people you have relationships with. It is important that people give each other space and opportunity to share their thoughts and feelings.

Communication is a two-way process: You can talk, but so too can the person you are in a relationship with.

Defining Relationship Skills: Communication

Effective communication involves more than just speaking well. Actually, good communication involves both speaking and listening well. If you want to communicate well with others, you need to do both. When you listen well, you pay attention to what someone is saying and try to understand their perspective. When you talk well, you express your thoughts, feelings, and needs clearly but with respect for the feelings of others.

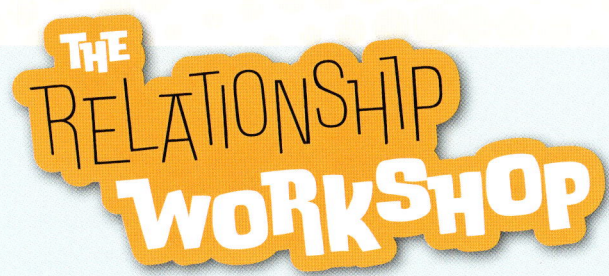

A Communication Breakdown

If your communication skills aren't great, it can really affect your relationships. Imagine this scenario: You have a problem that is eating away at you. Last week, you blurted out to your friends that your best friend is having issues at home with their family. Your friend had asked you not to say anything, but it just came out. They have since found out and are really upset. They shout, "You shouldn't have said anything!" You get upset, and shout back, "I couldn't help it. You shouldn't have told me if you don't want anyone to know." Since then, you and your friend haven't spoken. You want to talk to them—they are your best friend. But you don't know where to start.

> There is a problem with communication here. Your friend was hurt by your actions, but you didn't respond well. With better communication, the situation could be handled a lot better. Let's take a look overleaf.

The Relationship Workshop

Same situation, but with better communication.

Communicating Well

When your friend discovers that you have told others about their family issues, you can see they are very hurt. You realize that you have upset them. So you tell them, "I'm so sorry, I know you told me about your family in confidence, and I shouldn't have said anything. I just blurted it out without thinking. I should have been far more careful." You promise to take more care over what you say about your friend in the future—after all, they're your best friend. You give them a hug. Both of you feel relieved—your friendship is good again.

What Works Better Here?:

- You accept responsibility for having done something wrong, and apologize.
- You communicate calmly and clearly, without shouting and getting angry.
- You agree to be more sensitive in the future, and your friendship is repaired.

Effective Communication —What Can It Do for You?

Have you ever been in a situation like this? How did you communicate? Did it work out OK or could you have expressed yourself better? What have you learned and what would you do differently if a similar situation comes up in the future? In a conflict situation, there is real potential for it to blow up and get out of hand. Good communication is so important in these scenarios, because it helps defuse them and helps everyone calm down.

Good communication prevents misunderstandings and misinterpretations.

A PROBLEM-BUSTING TOOL

Seeing Things from Both Sides

Communication is really important for solving problems. When both people communicate well they can look at a problem from both sides, discuss what has gone wrong, and come up with solutions and decisions that work for both parties.

STUDIES IN TEEN SURVIVAL

Studies show that the quality of communication in a relationship is a good indicator of how healthy it is. Poor communication is linked to long-term problems and relationship breakdowns. People who communicate well and often in their relationships are usually happier in them.

Why Relationship Skills Work

Just as you'd use the correct tools to fix a car, managing relationships is all about using the right tools for the job. Let's take another look at the value of communication.

1. Good Communication Builds Understanding

Effective communication builds understanding between people, allowing them to consider each other's thoughts, feelings, needs, and perspectives.

2. Talking Solves Problems

Open and honest communication is a problem-busting power tool! Use it to get over disagreements in a constructive way.

3. Building Trust Repairs Relationships

If you talk honestly and explain yourself well, people will be more likely to understand why you may have made a mistake if you do make one, and trust that you will do your best to not make it again.

4. Communicating Builds Bonds

Communicating well builds connections between people in relationships and strengthens bonds.

Remember to Adapt and Grow

Relationships change, and that's OK. Understanding that your relationships will evolve is half the battle in managing them. As long as you keep talking with the people you care about, you'll be able to navigate changing needs, thoughts, and feelings as you go.

CHAPTER 2
You and Your Family: A Survival Guide

Managing family relationships can be tricky, and never more so than when you are a teen. For a start, you have a LOT going on, and emotions can be pretty much all over the place. Throw parents/caregivers and brothers and sisters into the mix and family life can feel like a boiling pot of bubbling emotions.

What Your Parents Think

You and your parents may well have very different views when it comes to behavior, responsibilities, and decision making. You think one thing, they think another—and likely you find it hard to get to a middle ground. It may help to try and remember that your parents may be having a tough time letting go. After all, they've spent all your childhood making decisions for you and making sure you are safe and cared for. Come the teenage years, that starts to slip away—and that can feel pretty scary for a parent.

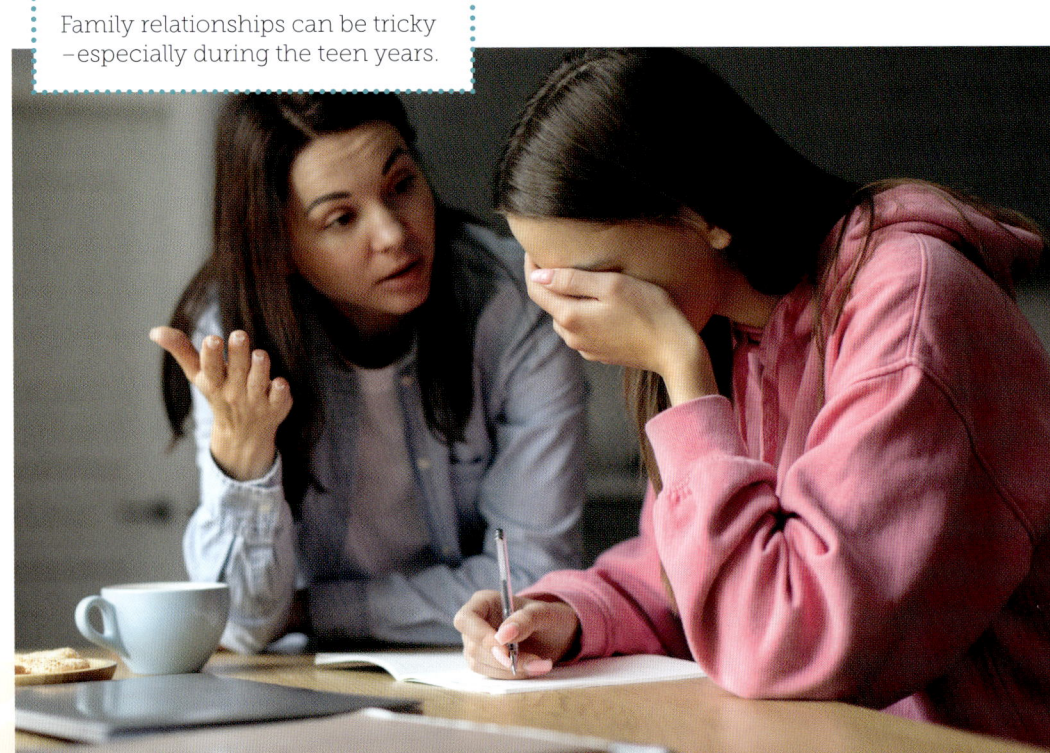

Family relationships can be tricky—especially during the teen years.

What You Think

Meanwhile, you are trying to find your feet, learn who you are and what you like, and beginning to strike out into the world on your own. For you too, life can feel pretty scary sometimes, as well as exciting. With all this change, things can become very fraught at home.

You may clash with your parents over school, friends, interests, future goals, clothes, food—pretty much anything! Then, there may also be siblings in the mix. They may be older, younger, or in their teens too. You may find them annoying sometimes, fun at others, or you just may not want to spend that much time with them on occasion.

It's OK to Mess Up

Whatever your family set-up, it is going to be a lot easier getting along with everyone if you work on your relationship skills. You'll feel more in control if issues do arise, and your family members are the very best people with whom to start trying out relationship-management skills. Why? If you mess up at first, they'll easily forgive you and you can try again. And they are going to be in your life for a long time, so it makes sense to try and make your relationships with them as good as they can be. So, let's get on board with the next two relationship skills: conflict resolution and compromise.

Conflict resolution and compromise are hard-hitters when it comes to navigating family relationships.

Teen Need to Know

Of teens aged 12 to 17, 81 percent say that they and their family talk about problems, work together to solve them, and keep positive even when times feel hard.

Parents are not perfect, and sometimes they may get angry and shout. If you can keep calm in that situation, it will help to stop it getting out of control.

Let's Talk about Conflict Resolution

Conflict resolution is incredibly important in healthy relationships. Let's face it, most people have disagreements from time to time. Some relationships may have them a lot, others only occasionally, but pretty much every relationship will experience conflict of some sort. Disagreements are all part of being human—after all, the world would be a boring place if we all agreed on everything. The key is to accept that disagreements will arise and learn how to manage them when they do.

Defining Relationship Skills: Conflict Resolution

Conflict resolution does not mean shouting the loudest so other people give up the argument and end it! While it's a fact of life that there will always be conflict in relationships, the way conflict is managed can lead to a good outcome or a really bad one. Good conflict resolution means finding a constructive and mutually agreeable end to an argument in which both parties can walk away feeling that they have been heard. It doesn't mean they need to agree, but maybe just that they agree to disagree. Conflict resolution means being able to put yourself in someone else's shoes, say you understand their emotions and respect them, and respond to their arguments with consideration.

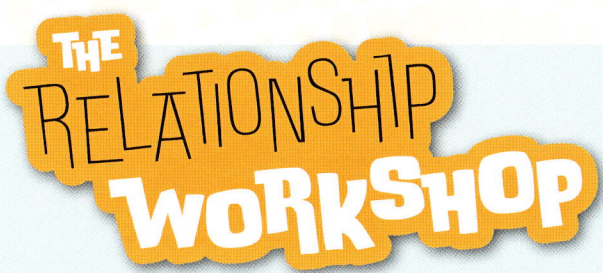

The Relationship Workshop

Headlong into Conflict

Conflicts are always going to come up in relationships, but how you deal with them makes all the difference to the outcome. Let's take a look at what happens when a conflict isn't resolved well.

Imagine you have a math test looming, and your dad is insisting that you spend more of your free time studying. "It pays to put the work in now," he says, again! You roll your eyes. Your dad is obsessed with school and getting good grades, but you know for a fact he flunked school. "When did you put in the work?" you laugh. That makes him mad. He shouts, "Trust me. I wish I'd spent more time working and less time partying at your age." You storm out the house. You wish your dad would just back off, stop nagging, and leave you alone.

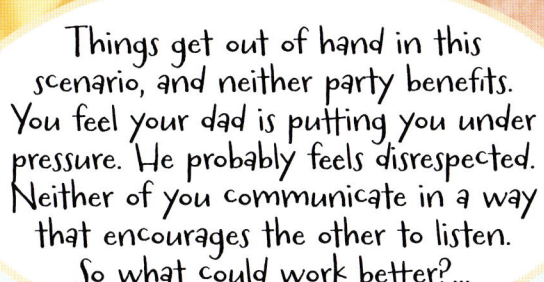

Things get out of hand in this scenario, and neither party benefits. You feel your dad is putting you under pressure. He probably feels disrespected. Neither of you communicate in a way that encourages the other to listen. So what could work better?...

▶ ▶ ▶

The Relationship Workshop

Same situation, but with less conflict.

Using Conflict Resolution

When your dad insists that you study instead of going out, you see he is worried, so you sit down. You guess you can listen for a minute. It's better than having a fight. "Look," he says, "I get that you want to have fun. I just wish I'd tried harder at school, and I want the best for you." You can see your dad cares, so you nod. "How about you do an hour of revision now, then go out after?" he suggests. You think about it. "Just one hour!" you reply. "Deal!" your dad smiles back.

What Works Better Here?:

- You give your dad a chance to talk, and choose to listen carefully to his thoughts.
- A middle ground is found—an hour's revision.
- The situation is defused and both people find a solution they are happy with.

Conflict Resolution— What Can It Do for You?

When people really listen to someone else, it can help defuse a conflict, because the other person feels that their concerns are being heard.

When someone gives another person their full attention when they are speaking, makes and maintains eye contact, nods, and uses other nonverbal clues to show that they are paying attention, they are listening actively.

A PROBLEM-BUSTING TOOL

Active Listening

Has anyone ever told you that you aren't listening to them, even when you think you are? Maybe you weren't giving them your full attention, perhaps you were looking at your phone as you were listening to them, or watching TV. If people don't feel listened to, it can be very upsetting. It often makes them feel that no one cares about them. Active listening is important in a relationship because it makes people feel valued and respected.

Step this way for more great ways to listen well. ▶▶▶

Other Ways to Listen

People can listen well in different ways in relationships. They include:

- **Empathetic listening:** When you put yourself in another person's shoes and try to understand their perspective and emotions, you are listening empathetically.
- **Reflective listening:** Repeating or summarizing what another person has said shows that you understand their message. This is reflective listening.
- **Nonverbal listening:** People use facial expressions, body language, and different tones of voice when they are talking. Good listeners pay attention to these cues, because they give messages about what someone is thinking and feeling.

The Value of Listening

Have you ever felt really bored with listening? Did you want to go and do something else? Perhaps you didn't like what you heard and preferred to switch off? Listening can sometimes feel like hard work.

While you might not enjoy listening to what your parents, siblings, or other family members have to say, that doesn't mean you shouldn't try. You wouldn't like it if they didn't listen to you! When you actively listen to people, they are less likely to get angry, because they can see they have your full attention and the message they have to give is being heard. Active, empathetic, reflective, and nonverbal listening are also great tools to have in nonconfrontational situations too, so work on them—it will pay off.

STUDIES IN TEEN SURVIVAL

Good connections between parents and children plays a big part in health and wellbeing. When there are close and positive family relationships, in which people have open, effective communication, the teens in those families tend to keep healthier and avoid substance abuse, such as using drugs and alcohol. They are less likely to smoke or vape. Teens with healthy family relationships are less likely to have mental health issues and get into violent relationships outside the home.

How teens interact with their family members affects their lives long after the teen years have ended, too. Studies show that positive, healthy relationships with family members also make it more likely that teens will have better relationships with others when they grow up. Teens who develop healthy relationships with their family members are also less likely to suffer from mental health issues, such as depression and anxiety, throughout their adult lives.

The next time you feel that you are going to burst, try to pause and take a breath.

A Problem-Busting Tool

Take a Breath

Have you heard the phrase, "Stop and take a breath?" It is often used when people are very upset and angry. When you get really angry, it can be hard to think straight. You might blurt out hurtful words in the heat of an argument, and regret them later. You might shout or throw things around. All these behaviors do nothing to resolve conflicts, but usually just make them worse. If you recognize that you feel very upset, angry, and possibly unable to control what you say and do, stop. Then, calmly tell the person you are unhappy with that you want to take some space to think things through. That can often be the best way to manage the situation.

Let's Talk about Compromise

Families today are not what they were 20, 30, or 50 years ago. Things have changed—a lot. These days, families can take many different shapes. Children might live with both parents, or one parent if there has been a separation or divorce. They may spend part of their time with both parents or live solely with one. They may have a stepparent, stepbrothers, and stepsisters. Some children may live with their grandparents, others may live with foster parents for a while.

Whatever the family dynamics, the same key relationship skills will be needed, and compromise is one that applies to every family. This powerful relationship skill allows people to overcome conflict situations in which neither person wants to give ground.

Defining Relationship Skills: Compromise and Flexibility

Compromise and flexibility are must-have relationship skills. That's because unless you want to be at loggerheads with other people all the time (and that would be pretty exhausting), you are going to have to find some common ground. Compromise simply means adjusting what you want a little so other people feel they are getting something too. Being flexible means being willing to make changes if necessary, to make sure other people in a relationship are also happy. These are key skills you will need for life in your relationships, so it makes sense to start working on them now.

Sometimes, people feel really passionate about something and believe that they should not have to give up what they want. But having relationships means that we must consider the feelings of other people, and that can mean giving a bit of ground to keep things healthy and happy.

STUDIES IN TEEN SURVIVAL

Studies of families show that it's not realistic or likely to expect family relationships to be smooth all the time. In fact, all research points to the fact that families are likely to experience rifts and difficulties. However, how people respond to them is the key in whether those rifts have positive or negative outcomes. Some studies of parents and children have shown that even in relationships that are considered healthy and happy, parents and children are only in sync, or relating happily to each other, about 30 percent of the time. The remaining 70 percent, they may experience issues that need to be resolved so that they can move back toward a more harmonious state.

The evidence shows that while family arguments might be hard to deal with, they help children learn to manage their relationships, manage problems, and become more resilient as a result. Learning that relationships can be tricky is all part of discovering that things do not always run smoothly, and that overcoming issues is part of managing daily life. As long as parents and children quickly resolve their differences and repair the relationships, the learning process is a healthy one.

The Benefits of Compromise

When you feel that you don't want to compromise, or don't think that you should, take a step back from the situation and look at it again. Think about what you have to gain from compromising, rather than what you have to lose. The benefits of compromise are huge:

- People in relationships trust others who show they are willing to compromise.
- Compromise reduces conflict, which means you are less likely to continue with an argument and can move back to getting on well with others again.
- Compromise shows you are willing to be flexible, which means others, in turn, are likely to be more flexible with you.
- Your relationships are more likely to be fair and equal if you are willing to compromise.

Overall, compromising is essential for keeping your relationships happy and harmonious.

> When you really don't feel like compromising, try to think about how much happier you will be if your relationships feel good, and the compromise will seem worth making.

A Skill for Life

You'll come across plenty of situations in life in which you will need to problem-solve, and knowing how to compromise is a great skill to have when it comes to negotiating with others. If you can show willingness to compromise, and have the skills to do so, you'll be ahead of the game when it comes to navigating the rest of your life.

Compromise is often a key part of working life when negotiating with colleagues.

STUDIES IN TEEN SURVIVAL

Did you know that how you relate to your siblings, if you have them, can have a direct effect on your wellbeing? Studies by psychologists have shown that how siblings behave with each other teaches them how to relate to people outside their family. When siblings provide each other with mutual support, those children are more likely to find it easy to form friendships and other relationships in adolescence, and then later in adulthood. Having supportive siblings can also help children and teens who might be experiencing bullying at school or college or who have relationship problems with their parents.

Likewise, how you relate to siblings can also have a detrimental effect on your wellbeing and relationships with people outside the family. Studies show that siblings who abuse substances, such as drinking alcohol and taking drugs, have a negative effect on their brothers and sisters, and make them more likely to use drugs and alcohol too.

A lot of conflict between siblings can also have a negative effect on mental wellbeing, with teens more likely to experience mental health issues such as depression as a result of conflict. That conflict can include a lot of aggressive arguments and bullying or belittling siblings. People are also more likely to act out that kind of behavior in their own relationships outside the family too if they experience it within the family dynamic.

Why Relationship Skills Work

This chapter has been all about learning how to manage relationships in your family, but all the skills you've discovered will apply to every relationship you'll have. Let's take another look at the value of conflict resolution and compromise.

1. Resolving Conflicts Helps You Listen to Others

Conflict resolution allows you to listen actively to another person's perspective and concerns. That helps you gain a better understanding of their needs and views.

2. You Can Fix Problems with Compromise

Compromise helps solve problems, so that you can move on and get back to a happier and healthier relationship.

3. Talking Helps You Clear the Air

When problems aren't faced and talked about, they fester. People may become more and more resentful of others, and the relationship deteriorates. Talking about and resolving any issues helps you clear the air.

4 Overcoming Differences Helps You Build Connections

People who can quickly resolve their differences are more likely to feel connected to each other.

5 Speaking Openly Builds Trust

Knowing that you can speak openly in a relationship and share your concerns makes it more likely that you will trust others, and they in turn will trust you.

In It for the Long Term

Learning how to resolve problems and communicate well will help make sure your relationships are strong and able to withstand future problems. And you'll also be able to carry these key skills into your future.

CHAPTER 3

School, College, and Work

We've talked about managing relationships within families and a little about managing friendships too. But there are other large parts of life in which navigating how you relate to others is equally important—school, college, and work. And the relationship skills you'll learn while in education will help set you up for managing relationships at work.

Skilled for School, Skilled for Life

School and college life throw up all sorts of relationship issues. That includes managing friendships, navigating people you may not like or get on well with, and dealing with people in authority.

In this part of your life, you'll learn more communication, conflict resolution, and compromise skills. Communicating well with people you work with is very important. If you can communicate effectively, you can share your ideas and discuss problems. Being able to resolve conflicts also helps defuse situations that come up in an educational or work setting. For example, you may not agree with a classmate who is working with you on a school project. In that scenario, you'll need to be able to share your thoughts in a calm and constructive way, and be better able to resolve any issues that come up.

> You are always going to have to compromise when other people are involved in a project or joint venture in the world of work. They will have their own ideas about how things should be done, so you'll need to find some middle ground.

When you are self-aware, you'll find it easier to communicate your wants and needs to others, which will improve your relationships. So get to know yourself inside and out!

Getting to Know You!

Your school and college years are also a great time to work on another important relationship—your relationship with yourself. That's right, it's not just how you relate to other people that is important, how you relate to yourself is equally key. Learning to be self-aware means developing an awareness of who you are. That includes what you like and what you don't like, what your strengths and weaknesses are, what is important to you and what is less meaningful, and so on.

Teen Need to Know

Studies show that people who are self-aware perform better at school and work, get more promotions, and are more effective leaders.

Getting to Grips with New Tools

As you move through your school, college, and work life, you'll need to develop more relationship tools. These will include assertiveness, collaboration, and empowerment. These are skills that will help you build relationships with the people you work with. In this chapter, we'll take a look at these powerful tools.

Let's Talk about Being Assertive

Remember our list of ten key relationship skills? Number four is assertiveness. This powerful skill can help you get the most out of your experiences in education and in work. Assertiveness in relationships means that people are mutually respectful of each other, honest, and build a sense of trust. Assertiveness helps people communicate healthily and establish boundaries. It builds strong and fulfilling relationships in which everyone feels heard and valued. It is a skill that will help you feel assured in putting forward what you want and need.

> Assertiveness is valuable in relationships in workplace and educational settings, and in personal relationships too.

Defining Relationship Skills: Assertiveness

Do you think that being assertive means being the loudest voice in the room and putting your needs before others? Actually, being assertive does not mean throwing your weight around. People who are assertive express their ideas and feelings in a confident way, but with consideration for the rights and feelings of others. Being assertive means standing up for yourself, but doing so without being overly aggressive. When someone is assertive, they stand their ground in a firm-but-respectful way and make it clear to others that they will not be bullied or disrespected.

Lacking Assertiveness

Teens and young people have to navigate relationships with fellow students and teachers in education, and assertiveness often comes into play. Let's take a look at a scenario in which it is an important skill.

Imagine you are in the school drama club. A part in a play comes up, and you'd love to try out for it. When the drama teacher asks for a raise of hands for the part, you put yours up. But so does your friend! Then they whisper to you, "I really want this part, couldn't you try for another? I'd have a much better chance of getting it if you don't go for it too."

You don't think that's fair. After all, you want the part just as much as they do. But you shrug your shoulders, and say, "OK." Afterward, you feel really disappointed. You think you would have been great in that role, and you wish you'd stood your ground.

Considering the needs of others is always important, but so is considering your own wants too. Being assertive would have made a big difference in this situation, without causing upset to others...

THE RELATIONSHIP WORKSHOP

Same situation, but with assertiveness.

Considering Yourself

In drama club, when your friend asks you to step away from the part, it doesn't really seem fair. After all, you want the part just as much as they do. So you say, "Let's both try out for it. We both stand a good chance, and then the drama teacher can choose who gets the part. I really want to give it a go—it means a lot to me too." Your friend says, "OK. I get it." You feel good that they understand, and that you will get a chance to try out for the part.

What Works Better Here?:

- You are assertive, and explain to your friend that the part means a lot to you too.
- You suggest a plan that will work for you both.
- Afterward, you feel good that you have given yourself a chance and did not give up what you wanted just to make someone else happy.

Assertiveness—What Can It Do for You?

Have you ever been in a situation like this? Did you not speak up for yourself? Did it work out OK or could you have expressed yourself better? Assertiveness is very important in these types of situations—if someone doesn't know what you feel, think, and want, how can they respond to it?

Assertiveness paves the ground for setting boundaries and letting others know what you are happy to accept.

A Problem-Busting Tool

Express Yourself

Being assertive is all about being confident with expressing your thoughts and feelings. It means telling others about what you want and where your boundaries lie in a respectful way that also considers their feelings. Assertiveness is right in the middle between being passive, or not speaking up for yourself, and being aggressive, which means being too pushy about what you want. Being assertive means your voice is heard in a relationship, and others respect you for it.

Let's Talk about Collaboration

Have you ever worked on something with a friend or group of friends that you enjoyed? It could have been a project at school or something outside of school, such as a game of baseball or soccer. Maybe the group project was making some jewelry or a piece of art. Perhaps you were in a band or a music group, and worked together to create a piece of music. Whatever the project, you will have collaborated. One of the great things about working with other students on a project at school or college is the chance to collaborate.

Working with others is one of the features that many people look for when they go to work, and that they value in their career. Collaboration is a key part of the world of work, and learning this important skill while in education can set you up for a happy and productive future career.

> If your teacher suggests working collaboratively, give it a go.

Collaboration is why organizations often send their staff on team-building activities. It might seem like just a bit of fun, but it actually helps create positive relationships between coworkers. That then helps them function better back in the workplace.

Defining Relationship Skills: Collaboration

Collaboration means working with others as part of a team to get the best possible result. When people collaborate, they bring all their many joint skills to the table to improve the outcome of a project or shared piece of work. Have you ever heard the saying, "Two heads are better than one?" It's often used to describe the best way to problem-solve: Trying to do it alone can be really hard, but when you get another person on board, they have a new perspective, new ideas, and new solutions to throw into the pot. When you work collaboratively, or as a team, it's like having another brain on the job—or two, three, four, or more brains! Collaboration can also make work a lot more fun.

Why Collaboration Feels Good

Working as a team has so many benefits for people: It helps them lean on each other's strengths and skills while also giving them the chance to develop skills of their own. It creates a sense of camaraderie, in which all people work together for a common goal. It helps build connections between people, which makes them work together more effectively on future projects too. Collaboration makes workplaces productive.

Learning to Collaborate

We've already learned a lot of the skills that people need to collaborate well. Let's recap them here:
- **Active listening:** Listening properly to what team members are saying means you take on board their thoughts and different perspectives.
- **Good communication:** Speaking clearly about what you think helps others understand your perspective and thoughts.
- **Conflict resolution:** Remaining calm if a conflict does come up, and trying to find a solution that suits everyone, helps keep a team strong.

Other important skills that also come into play when working well as a team include:
- **Setting clear goals and expectations:** Knowing what the goal of a project is and what you expect to achieve is key when working as a team. Communicating this fully from the outset means everyone is on board before the project begins. And if you are made a team leader at any point, you will need to be able to effectively explain goals and objectives to your team from the outset.
- **Being able to adapt:** Adaptation is key when working with other people. Things may change as you work, or problems may come up that mean you need to change course.
- **Valuing diversity:** Appreciating that everyone is different is a real strength. In fact, it's the differences in people that have made humans so successful. When a group has a lot of different individuals within it, it means they all have particular skills to bring to a project. If everyone was the same, their strengths and skills would be the same—and that would leave huge gaps of knowledge. Differences should be celebrated.

Being able to adapt and change is very important—if you keep an open mind, you will be more willing and able to consider new ideas from other people.

Learning to value differences in others will mean that you recognize their worth and will encourage the contribution that other people have to make.

How to Join In

People sometimes find it difficult to join in with collaborative projects. They may feel shy and that no one will want to listen to what they have to say. If that sounds like you, try watching how others behave collaboratively, and then model their behavior to help you learn how to work in a group. Try asking questions, listening to others, and offering a different perspective. Taking small steps to start with can help build confidence until you feel happy to make a full contribution.

STUDIES IN TEEN SURVIVAL

Finding opportunities to practice collaboration can help people work on this skill in a low-key, nonstressful environment. Try looking for collaborative projects, team activities such as sports groups, and community or volunteer projects. They are great ways to get involved with teams and learn to contribute to a group.

Let's Talk about Empowerment

Having the confidence to share your thoughts and feelings is a powerful asset. However, teens may not always feel confident about having "a voice," perhaps fearing that their thoughts and feelings won't be taken seriously or given validation. Feeling empowered about speaking up in relationships outside your family can seem daunting at first, but it is a really great skill to have. Empowerment means that you can go out into the world sure that you can speak your mind and encourage others to listen to your views.

> If both people in a relationship feel empowered, that relationship is likely to be far more balanced and healthy.

Defining Relationship Skills: Empowerment

Some people might think that empowerment means feeling all-powerful and having complete control over others. Actually, empowerment means feeling confident in your thoughts, choices, and decisions but also supporting others to feel confident in their thoughts, choices, and decisions too. When people in relationships feel empowered, they feel that they have a voice and can openly discuss any issues they may have with others. That means that any problems are quickly aired and discussed, and then easily resolved.

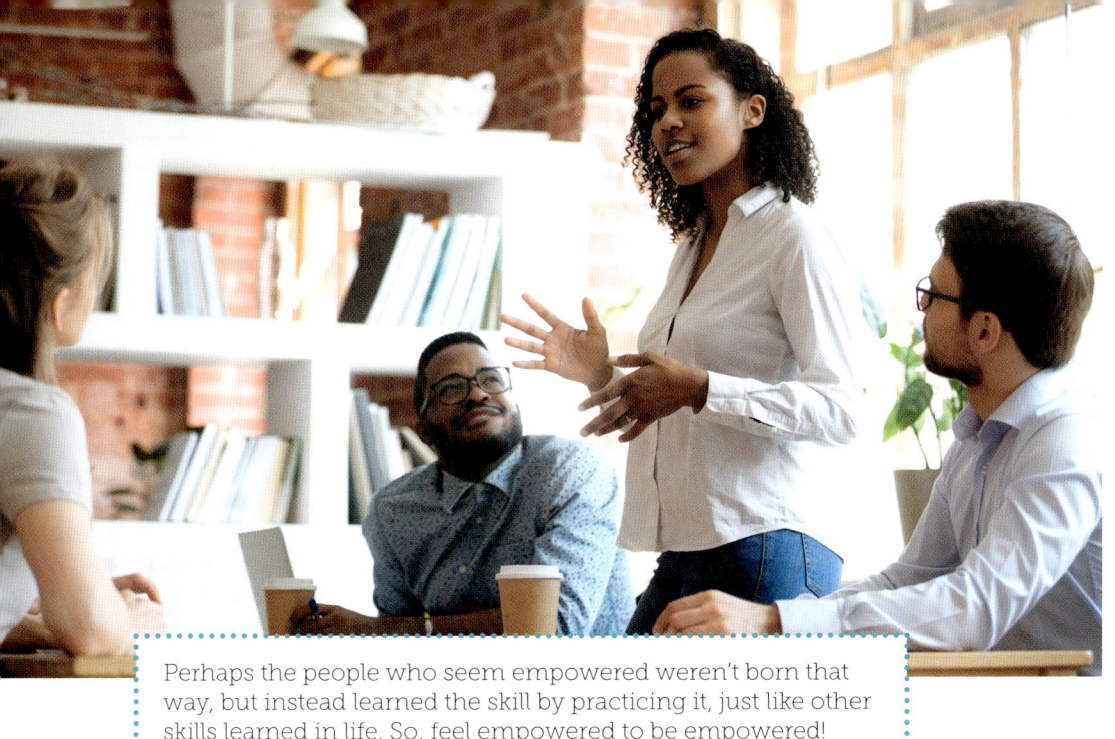

Perhaps the people who seem empowered weren't born that way, but instead learned the skill by practicing it, just like other skills learned in life. So, feel empowered to be empowered!

Learning to Be Empowered

People who are empowered feel more self-confident and able to communicate their thoughts, feelings, and boundaries. They are more likely to join in discussions with friends, teachers, and other students at school or college. And later in life, they are more likely to find it easy to work with coworkers and employers. Being empowered means:

- **Communicating assertively:** Speaking up firmly about what you believe in, while allowing others to do so too
- **Being confident about making decisions:** Feeling sure that you have the ability to make decisions about your life and future, and follow through on them
- **Feeling able to problem-solve:** Believing that you have the tools to overcome adversity, and using those tools in challenging situations
- **Being able to lead:** Feeling that you have the skills to lead a group of people and motivate them to complete tasks.

Although some people seem to be born with confidence, empowerment doesn't come overnight for many. Those people may find it more difficult to feel empowered. Working on this skill and practicing it can help build empowerment.

Why Relationship Skills Work

You've discovered skills that will see you through school, college, and into your career: assertiveness, collaboration, and empowerment. Let's take one more look at their value.

1. Assertiveness Builds Confidence

People who are assertive are confident about expressing themselves in relationships and allowing others to do the same. That encourages open communication and quick problem-solving.

2. Collaboration Encourages Diversity

Recognizing the contribution that everyone has to make because of their differences creates more dynamic and productive groups, and helps everyone showcase their unique abilities.

3. Adaptability Helps Manage Change

Being able to be flexible as situations change allows you to consider others' different and changing viewpoints without difficult confrontations arising that seem impossible to resolve.

4
Teamwork Is Enriching

Learning to work effectively as part of a team ensures that your relationships with people outside of your family are healthy and happy and you flourish in work environments.

5
Empowerment Helps You Share

Building your confidence in yourself and your capabilities allows you to speak up in group situations, share thoughts, and respectfully listen to the viewpoints of others.

Remember to Work on Yourself

Getting to know yourself, your likes, dislikes, strengths, and weaknesses makes you a more well-rounded person who can better relate to others in working environments. So, keep working on your relationship with you.

CHAPTER 4

Friendships and the Wider World

Friendships are a wonderful thing, and friends are often incredibly important to teens and young adults. Friendships allow you to explore who you are outside of your family. Your friends probably see you very differently from how your family sees you. You might behave in an entirely different way around friends, feeling able perhaps to express parts of your personality that you might not so easily share at home. Friendships help you develop who you are as a person, and shape how you relate to people beyond your family unit for the rest of your life.

Becoming More Diverse

Beyond immediate friendships, how you relate to people you may not know as well in the wider world is very important, too. Today, we have connections with more people than ever thanks to the development of communication systems such as social media. Our society is more diverse, made up of people from many different backgrounds and many different cultures. We are more connected than ever.

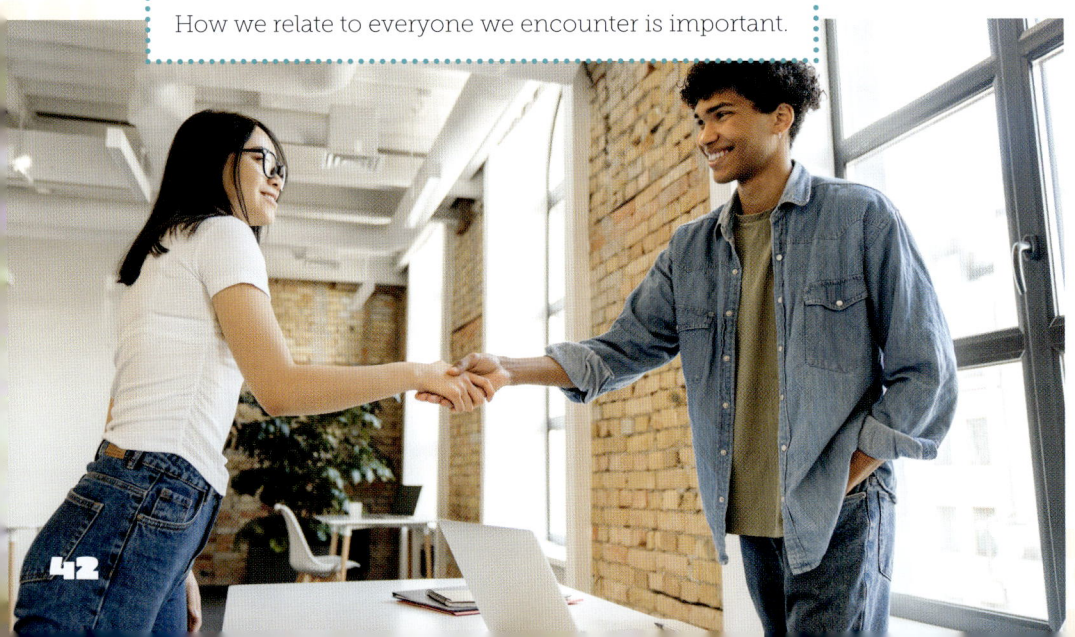

How we relate to everyone we encounter is important.

We should treat everyone with the same level of respect, tolerance, and compassion that we expect others to give us.

Still a Way to Go

However, despite a more diverse society, attitudes toward diversity are not always healthy. Racial attitudes can be biased, with Black, Asian, Latino, and other ethnic minorities experiencing racism. Gender attitudes can be biased too, with women experiencing discrimination.

Relating to Differences

As you work your way through life, you are going to come across a lot of different people—and that's a great thing! By meeting many different types of people, you'll discover more about the world. That includes different cultures and many different beliefs—all the things that make our planet home to so many amazingly diverse people.

By keeping an open, enquiring mind that celebrates and welcomes diversity, you'll relate healthily to different people when you meet them, and feel enriched by doing so. Relating to people in the wider world in a respectful and inclusive way is one of the most important skills you can learn. And that leads us to the final skills our list: empathy, tolerance, respect, and trust-building.

Teen Need to Know

Young Americans are becoming more diverse than ever. The US Census Bureau's latest data shows that half of Americans under the age of 16 identify as a racial or ethnic minority.

Let's Talk about Empathy

Have you ever felt sad about something, and shared how you felt with a friend or family member? How did they react to you? Did they put an arm around your shoulder or give you a hug? Perhaps they told you that they understand how you feel, that they had felt the same way too, and that everything will be OK. If they did, they were showing you empathy. And have you done the same for someone you care about when they have been struggling? If you have, then you have shown empathy too.

Empathy is an amazingly powerful relationship tool. When you are empathetic to a friend, family member, or even a complete stranger, it can make a huge difference to how they feel.

Defining Relationship Skills: Empathy

Empathy is feeling sad when others feel sad, right? Not quite. Empathy sounds a little like sympathy, and it's not far off. But empathy really means trying to understand and share the feelings of others. It's a little like putting yourself in their shoes and imagining how that might feel. It's letting someone know that you understand how they feel, that it's OK to feel like that, and showing them compassion. Sometimes, people just need to know that you get it—you understand, and that you are OK with them saying they are not OK. It's often a big weight off for that person and can make them feel a lot better.

THE RELATIONSHIP WORKSHOP

A Lack of Empathy

Being able to show empathy can change the way another person feels and help them deal with their emotions. It's a great skill to have, but sometimes, people can feel nervous or uncomfortable when others are upset. Imagine this scenario:

A new girl starts at your school, and she spends a lot of time alone. You learn that she has come from Syria, and her family are refugees. She looks lonely at lunch, so you walk over and introduce yourself. She smiles back, and looks pleased that you came over.

You get into conversation, and she tells you about her old life back in Syria. She had to leave behind her home, a lot of her family, and all of her friends. As she speaks, she looks really sad. You think she might cry. You don't know what you'll do if that happens, so you say, "Well, I'll catch up with you soon. I've got to head back into class now." Lunch isn't over, but you feel uncomfortable—what will you do if she gets emotional? You don't think you can handle it.

> Feeling uncomfortable in a situation can be a big barrier in showing empathy. But if you can overcome those feelings, you can reach out a friendly hand. Let's take a look...

THE RELATIONSHIP WORKSHOP

Same situation, but with empathy.

Empathy Builds Bonds

When you get into conversation with the new girl, she tells you about her life back in Syria. As she speaks, she looks really sad. You think she might cry. You don't know what you'll do if that happens. But you also think about how she must be feeling, and how you'd feel if you had to leave so much behind, like her. "It must have been so hard," you say, and squeeze her hand. She cries but you give her a hug and say, "You can hang out with me and my friends, now. I know it's not the same as having your old friends, but we'll be here for you."

What Works Better Here?:

- You put yourself in someone else's shoes, and think about how it must feel to give up so much. You realize how hard it must be.
- You show compassion and put another's feelings before your own.
- Although the new girl is emotional, you handle it. Now, the next time someone gets upset, you know you will cope just fine.

Empathy—What Can It Do for You?

Often, people just need a simple hug and a reassurance that you understand how they feel. Emotions are just emotions—everyone feels them. But when we face feelings, they stop being so scary, and we learn that we can handle them in others and ourselves. Empathy is a wonderful relationship tool, because it can be the support someone needs when they are really low. It feels good to help others feel better.

A PROBLEM-BUSTING TOOL

Gaining Trust and Understanding

Empathy is a skill that helps you understand and appreciate the experiences and feelings of others. Being empathetic to others builds trust in your relationships. If the people you care about feel that they can share their thoughts and emotions with you, and that you'll understand them, they will feel a bond and sense of closeness with you. If issues and problems then do come up, you'll be able to face them together.

By putting yourself in someone else's shoes, you'll gain a deeper understanding of different viewpoints and see the world from many different perspectives.

You Can Learn to Be Empathetic

Some people find it easier than others to be empathetic. That's not necessarily because they are more caring people, they may just find it easier to show that side of themselves. If you find it difficult to be empathetic, it helps to remember that empathy is a skill that can be learned. Start by thinking about how it might feel to be another person experiencing a difficulty. Then, when you are in a real-life situation that might require you to be empathetic, do the same—imagine yourself in that person's shoes. It will then be easier to show that person care and compassion because you can sense what it might be like to experience their situation.

Empathy Workshops

Bullying at school or college can be a real problem. There is no place for bullying in any situation, but unfortunately, bullying still goes on. And often, people who belong to an ethnic minority become the victims of bullies.

Today, some schools and colleges run empathy-building workshops in which students are encouraged to consider the thoughts and feelings of people who are being bullied because of their ethnicity. In the workshops, students create an empathy map to reflect the experience of a person being bullied. They do so by answering these questions about that person:
- What do they think?
- What do they feel?
- What do they say?
- What do they do?

Bullies victimize people that they feel they can single out, and then systematically abuse them either mentally, physically, or both.

Once they have completed their maps, students show them to the rest of the group. They then have a discussion about the emotional, physical, and social effect of the bullying.

Empathy maps help students by encouraging them to put themselves in the shoes of those who are being bullied. The maps encourage students to consider what it must be like to experience bullying. By doing so, students are able to feel a sense of empathy for those who are bullied, and the incidences of bullying in a school are less likely to occur as a result.

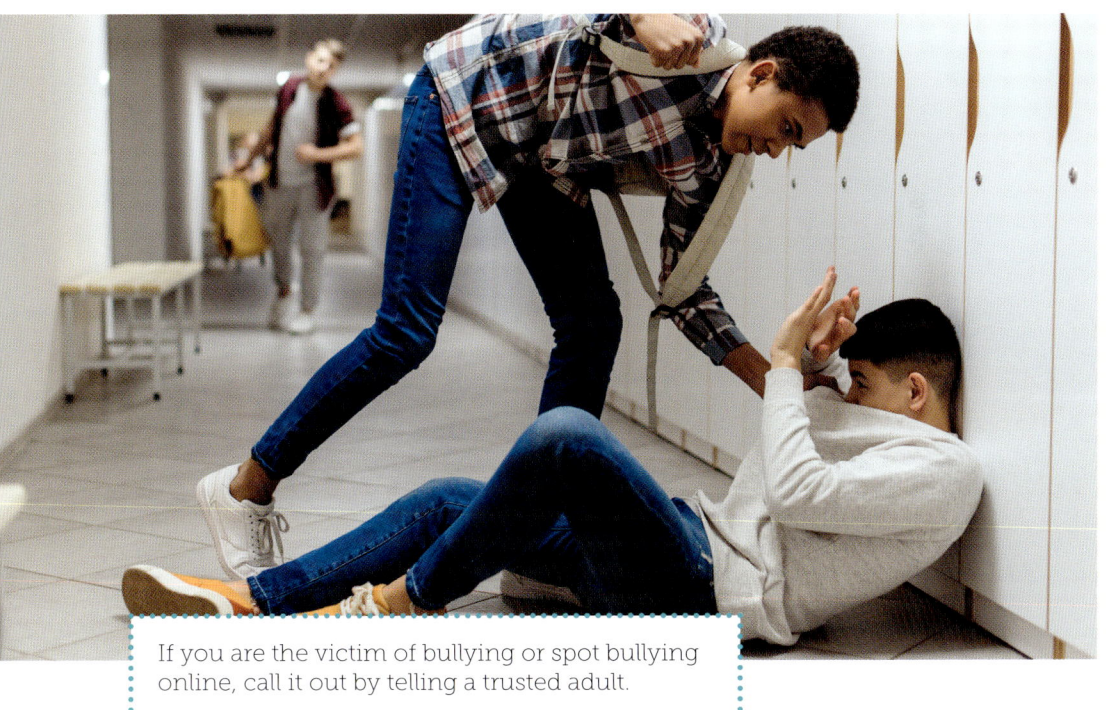

If you are the victim of bullying or spot bullying online, call it out by telling a trusted adult.

STUDIES IN TEEN SURVIVAL

Social media can be a great friendship tool. It helps people keep in touch with each other, share news and ideas, and have fun, all without needing to go anywhere at all. However, there is a downside too. Sometimes, messages posted online can be misleading—if you are not careful about how you write and what you say, it can be very easy to upset others. And then, of course, there are those who may want to upset others, and use social media as a place to bully. Just as bullying should not be tolerated in real life, it should not be tolerated in the virtual world either.

Let's Talk about Tolerance

In all your relationships, you are likely to need tolerance on a pretty regular basis. Unless you jet off into space to live alone on another planet, you are going to have to learn to tolerate others! Tolerance is a powerful relationship tool because it helps us manage how we respond to the behavior and characteristic traits of people we have relationships with.

> In a relationship, tolerance allows people to have interests, beliefs, and values that might be different from yours, but are respected. And vice versa, you may have ideas that are very different from the people you relate to, but they in turn accommodate them. Tolerance is a two-way street.

Defining Relationship Skills: Tolerance

Tolerance is a big word when it comes to relationships. In fact, pretty much any healthy relationship cannot work without tolerance. It means learning to be accepting of differences in others. You may not always like them, and they may really annoy you sometimes, but that's all part of a relationship. People are different from each other—you might love some of those differences. But others, not so much! But learning to live with differences without constantly pointing them out and complaining about them will lead to a much calmer and happier relationship.

STUDIES IN TEEN SURVIVAL

There can be a lot of pressure on teens to conform, or fit in with people around them. They may feel that they have to behave in the same way that some of their peers are doing, even if those behaviors aren't the best, such as singling out other people because of the way they look or if they have different interests. It can be tough not to join in with the crowd. But standing separately because of your values and beliefs feels far better than joining in with a group that is harmful toward others. And, sometimes, taking a stand helps others feel brave enough to follow your lead too.

A More Tolerant World

Tolerance is an invaluable part of relating to others, both within your close circle, such as family and friends, and outside of it among people you may not know very well. When people in a society are tolerant, there is less conflict and people live together more harmoniously. Let's take a look at all the plus points of tolerance:

- **Respecting differences:** Being tolerant of others no matter what their cultural background, personality traits, interests, or preferences
- **Being open-minded:** Being willing to listen to and respect other people's points of view, even if they are different from your own
- **Being flexible:** Being willing to adapt and change to accommodate other people.

Imagine if everyone was more tolerant—how do you think society would change? Do you think it would be greatly improved?

Tolerance means treating others with the consideration that you would expect them to give you.

Let's Talk about Respect

Respect. It's a big word, and it's used a lot. People often talk about not being respected, or not having any respect for others. They may demand respect from others. But what does respect really mean, and why is it important in relationships?

Respect Is Part of the Big Picture

Respect shows itself in many of the relationship skills that we've already covered in this book. From communication and conflict resolution to assertiveness and tolerance, respect is involved. Respect means valuing the boundaries of others and not crossing them. It means listening with attention to others and allowing them to speak their mind. It means being sensitive to other people's feelings, and showing that you can empathize. And it means allowing others to say they do not agree with you, then calmly and politely explaining your own viewpoint.

> ## Defining Relationship Skills: Respect
>
> Showing respect to others means valuing their opinions. You don't have to agree with them, but you do need to listen to them and let other people have them. It also means valuing people's feelings, and the boundaries that they might want to put in place.
>
> Sometimes, those boundaries may feel really annoying or silly, but they are *their* boundaries, so you need to respect them. For example, someone might not want to share their potato chips with you at lunchtime. You might think that is petty, even silly. But if they don't want to, *they don't want to*. By respecting the feelings, thoughts, and boundaries of other people, they'll be more inclined to respect yours too. Respect is incredibly important in relationships, so learn to respect this relationship skill!

Survival Tools

Respect is a word that your parents probably use a lot too, often when talking with you about boundaries and rules at home. They may say that you are "not respecting them," or that you "have no respect." That may make you angry, and you may not agree with them always. However, showing respect to others in your family and your home can make it a much better environment for everyone. Respect at home includes pitching in with chores such as cleaning. It can mean trying to be polite and courteous when talking to other family members. It means being responsible and accountable for all your actions.

Being respectful means being mindful of your parents' feelings and showing them consideration.

The Power of Respect

Friendships are much happier too when respect is at play. You can have fun with your friends. You can joke with each other, and tease each other about things. But knowing when to stop is important. It's all about boundaries. Knowing when a line should not be crossed, and staying the right side of it can help keep your friendships healthy. For example, you may have a friend who is very sensitive about their appearance. They may be unhappy with their skin, believe that it is zitty, and feel very self-conscious about it. If you joke about that, you are not respecting them and their feelings. They would be hurt and confused by your behavior, and that would in turn affect your friendship. When friends respect each other's ideas, feelings, and beliefs, they get along a lot better.

> When someone trusts you, they know you have their back.

Let's Talk about Trust

Trust, like respect, is another big word. People may talk about not having any trust in someone, or they may say that they trust you to do something. People can be described as "untrustworthy" or "trustworthy," but what does that really mean and what part does trust play in relationships? People often feel that trust is one of the most important aspects of a healthy relationship, and blame lack of trust for relationships breaking down. So what is trust, why is it so important, and how do people build it?

Defining Relationship Skills: Building Trust

Doesn't getting someone to trust you just mean convincing them you are telling the truth? Not quite. Building a person's trust means giving them good reason to believe that they can rely on you. It means they know they can come to you if they have a problem, or if they want to confide in you and don't want you to share what they have said. It means they know that if they need help, you'll do your best to give it. It means too that they feel safe enough to share really big emotions and thoughts with you, knowing that you won't judge them for it.

Trust is a really important theme in relationships—it's the bedrock for a great relationship.

How Do You Build Trust?

Getting people to trust you in a relationship often comes with time and certain actions. Your family trust you because you are related, but maintaining that trust is important, as is not taking it for granted. When trust is built in relationships people:

- **Communicate openly:** Having a lot of secrets and not sharing thoughts and feelings does not encourage others to trust you. Being open and sharing builds trust.
- **Are reliable:** When people know they can count on you to do something if you say you are going to do it, they trust you.
- **Respect others:** When you show respect for others' thoughts and feelings, they learn that they can trust you with them.
- **Understand boundaries:** Being respectful of other people's boundaries and not stepping over them will encourage them to put their trust in you. They will know you are reliable.

Trust Builds Better Workplaces

When it comes to workplace relationships, evidence shows that trust is as important as it is in nonworkplace relationships. Workplaces in which trust between colleagues is low have a much higher staff turnover, and the mental wellbeing of workers is much lower. When trust is present between people who work together, they are more likely to collaborate and work well.

Organizations in which levels of trust are high among colleagues are happier places, and workers are more likely to stay in their roles.

Why Relationship Skills Work

You made it to the end of the book and you've got some amazing skills to help steer you through your relationships. Let's revisit these last, valuable tools and what they can do for you once more: empathy, tolerance, respect, and trust-building.

1. Empathy Helps You Connect with People

When you show empathy to others, they will feel connected with you. That helps strengthen the bonds of a relationship.

2. Showing Respect Builds a Strong Relationship

When people respect each other, they allow the other person in a relationship to communicate openly, share their thoughts and views, and express their feelings. Being respectful means that boundaries are carefully maintained and people feel valued.

3. Tolerance Creates Fairness

A more tolerant approach to other people allows them to have space to be themselves. When people feel that they can express themselves and do the things they like, they are happier. And happier people create happier relationships.

4
Trust Makes Your Relationships Healthy

When people trust you, they are more likely to be honest and open with you. That will make your relationships far healthier.

Remember to Keep Learning

Working on relationship skills really is a lifelong process. No one gets it right all the time. People have slip-ups, and sometimes managing relationships can be hard. But don't throw in the towel! Just like every aspect of life, if you put in the work, the rewards will come. So, keep fine-tuning your relationship skills—you'll be glad that you did.

CONCLUSION
Skills for Life

Now that you are equipped with some amazing relationships skills, keep using them and practicing them as much as you can. Keep a note of how they help you and what works well. Consider what you think you could improve, and how your relationships feel as a result. And to set you on your way, here are some important guidelines to steer your course.

Don't Forget to Reflect!

Self-reflection will help you keep track of what you are thinking and feeling, and how that may be affecting your relationships.

Keep Talking

Honest, open communication is the key. Keep talking to the people you care about and keep sharing how you feel. If you share thoughts and emotions, you can deal with problems if they come up.

Self-reflection helps you check in with how you feel.

If you feel something, be sure to share it! Keep the communication flowing.

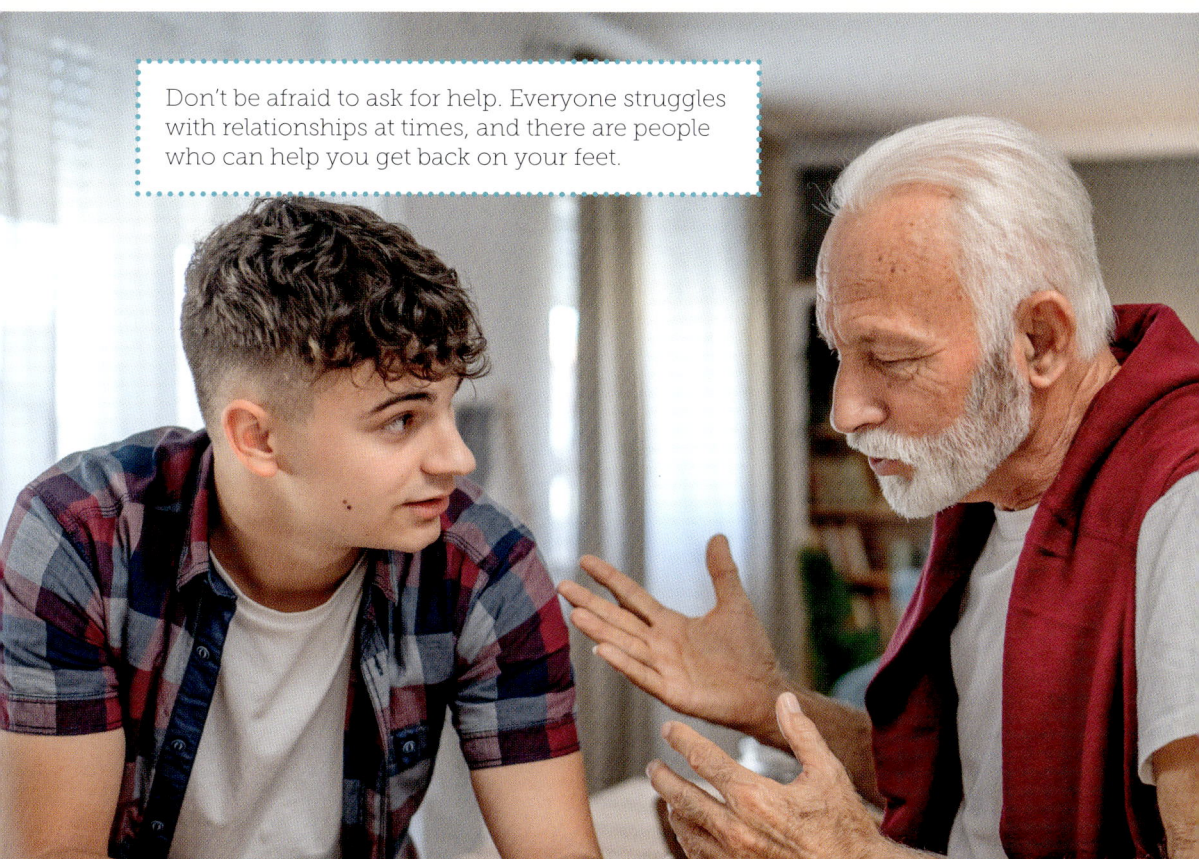

Don't be afraid to ask for help. Everyone struggles with relationships at times, and there are people who can help you get back on your feet.

If in Doubt, Ask

If you are unsure how to manage a relationship situation, ask a trusted adult to help. Your parents, teachers, and counselors are all there to help when the going gets tough. They will have had years of practice working on their relationship skills, so tap into their wealth of knowledge and many years of experience.

It's OK to Slip Up

No one has perfect relationships, and people slip up all the time. Just ask your parents and other adults—they will still be working on their relationship skills and they'll still make mistakes. But the good news is, with your newfound skills, you can get quickly back on track when you do make mistakes.

Share Your Skills

Don't keep your newfound skills to yourself, either! Remember to share what you've learned with friends and family. You've got some great tools under your belt now, and are in a position to help others better manage their relationships. And the more everyone is on board, the better all your relationships will be.

Glossary

abuse the harmful treatment of a person, such as hitting them or psychologically or sexually harming them

accountable taking responsibility for one's actions

adolescence the time of life when someone goes through the process of changing from a child into an adult

adversity hardship and difficulty

asset a benefit or positive feature

assured confident and certain

authority organizations that enforce rules

belittling making a person feel bad by ridiculing them, such as calling them names or criticizing them

benefit the advantage a person gains from something

biased having attitudes based on unfounded ideas, often about a person's race, social background, or gender

boundaries clear rules about things that are acceptable or unacceptable

camaraderie a sense of belonging, often gained by being part of a group

compassion kindness and care toward others

confide to tell someone something intimate and to trust them with that information

conflict argument and disagreement

consideration care for the feelings of others

constructive helpful and productive

courteous polite and respectful

cultures the beliefs, languages, and ways of behaving that are shared by a group of people

daunting seems overwhelming and very difficult

defuse to stop something becoming out of control, to calm a situation

depression a state of being very sad and having a lack of interest in the things that would normally be interesting

detrimental harmful

discrimination making judgments due to unfounded ideas about a person's race, social background, gender, or other defining characteristics

disrespected not shown respect

effective having a good and productive effect or outcome

enquiring wanting to learn more

ethnicity describes a person's race

evolve to develop and grow

express to show something

family dynamics the way that relationships within a family work

flexible able to easily bend and change

flourish to be successful

foster parents people who are not the biological parents of a child but who care for them for a while

gender a person's sex, such as male or female

harmonious in harmony, without conflict

hormone a chemical that sends messages around the body

identities ways that people perceive themselves

impulsive done quickly and often with little prior thought

in confidence told to someone believing they can be trusted with the information

inclusive not excluding others

motivate to be made to want to do something

mutual support the support that two people give each other

navigate to find the way

nonconfrontational without argument

nonverbal clues things that people learn about others by watching their facial expressions and body language rather than learning from what is said

peers people who are a similar age and who have similar experiences

perspectives viewpoints based on certain information

productive producing a lot and being constructive

psychologists professionals who study the human mind and the behaviors and thoughts of people

puberty the time of life during which a child changes into an adult

reassurance comfort and a feeling of security

regret a feeling of wishing that something had been different

relate how a person manages their relationship with others or gets on with other people

resilient having the ability to bounce back when something goes wrong

resolve to find a solution to a problem

siblings brothers and sisters

summarizing summing up

systematically in an ordered way

validation given worth

valued felt worthy and cared for

values things that are important to a person and in which they strongly believe

victimize to single someone out and cause them harm

Find Out More

BOOKS

Burling, Alexis. *Healthy Romantic Relationships*. Abdo Publishing, 2021.

Eason, Sarah. *Going Through a Family Breakup* (It Happened to Me). Cheriton Children's Books, 2022.

Honders, Christine. *The Ties that Bind Us Together* (Relationship Building). Rosen Publishing Group, 2020.

Nicks, Erin. *Developing Social Awareness*. BrightPoint Press, 2023.

WEBSITES

Visit the website of a helpful, nonprofit organization for information about social and emotional learning:
www.casel.org

Find out more about emotional wellbeing at:
www.cfchildren.org

ORGANIZATIONS

If you or someone you know needs help and support with relationship issues, help is available at this support service:

Teen Line, Cedars-Sinai, P.O.Box 48750, Los Angeles, CA 90048
(800) TLC-TEEN (852-8336)
Text TEEN to 839863
Website: teenline.org

Publisher's note to educators and parents:
All the websites featured above have been carefully reviewed to ensure that they are suitable for students. However, many websites change often, and we cannot guarantee that a site's future contents will continue to meet our high standards of educational value. Please be advised that students should be closely monitored whenever they access the Internet.

Index

abuse 20, 25, 48
adolescence 4, 25
adversity 39
assertiveness 5, 29–33, 40, 52

boundaries 30, 33, 39, 52–53, 55, 57
bullying 25, 48–49

collaboration 5, 29, 34–35, 37, 40
college 25, 28–29, 35, 39, 48
communication 5–6, 8–12, 20, 28, 36, 40, 42, 52, 58
compassion 43–44, 46, 48
compromise 5, 15, 22, 24–26, 28
conflict resolution 5, 15–16, 18, 26, 28, 36
consideration 16, 30, 51, 53
coworkers 35, 39
cultural backgrounds 51

different viewpoints 47
discrimination 43
diversity 36, 43

emotions 4, 6, 14, 16, 20, 45–47, 54, 58
empathy 5, 43–49, 56
empowerment 5, 29, 38–39, 41

families 20, 22–23, 28
friends 4, 15, 34, 39, 42, 45–46, 51, 53, 59

listening 7–8, 19–20, 36–37, 52

nonverbal clues 19

parents 4, 14–16, 20, 22–23, 25, 52–53, 59
puberty 4

relationship breakdowns 11
respect 5, 8, 16, 33, 43, 51–57

school 15, 17–18, 25, 28–29, 31, 34–35, 39, 45, 48–49
siblings 4, 15, 20, 25
social media 42, 49
substance abuse 20

teachers 31, 39, 59
tolerance 5, 43, 50–52, 56
trust 5, 12, 17, 24, 27, 30, 43, 47, 54–56

values 4, 50–51

work 4–6, 10–12, 15, 17–18, 20, 26, 28–30, 32, 34–37, 39–41, 43, 46, 50, 55–58

About the Author

Sarah Eason has written numerous books on many different topics, from science and history to space, geography, and social and emotional learning. She is the parent of two young adults, and hopes that this book helps other young people navigate the world of teen relationships, learn the tools they need to survive this sometimes-bumpy ride, and fly into adulthood skilled for life.